Visiting an
ANGLICAN CHURCH

Visiting an
ANGLICAN CHURCH

Susan Tompkins

Photography
NICK LOCKETT

Illustration/Design
JUDY BILLSON

LUTTERWORTH PRESS
CAMBRIDGE

Lutterworth Press
P.O. Box 60
Cambridge CB1 2NT

British Library Cataloguing in Publication Data available

First published in UK 1981 by Lutterworth Press
Reprinted 1983, 1988

I wish to thank the Rev. Denys Graebe, Vicar of St. George's, Norton, and his congregation for their help in compiling this book. I am also grateful to the many teachers and Church of England members who have read the manuscript and commented on it; and to Anne Pounds for the hours she has spent giving advice and proof reading.

When you look up the passages from the Bible remember that the first number after the name of the book is the chapter number, and the other numbers refer to the verses; so, Mark 15:22–37 is Mark's Gospel, chapter 15, verses 22 to 37. If the verse numbers are written 22, 37 it means verses 22 and 37.

ISBN 0-7188-2469-5

Picture on page 5 by Aerofilms Ltd., and on page 52 by The Papua New Guinea Partnership.

Printed in Great Britain by
St Edmundsbury Press Limited, Bury St Edmunds, Suffolk

Contents

1. Visiting a Church

What is a church? A **church** is a group of Christian people. It may be a small group or a large group: they may live in one place, or in different places all over the world. They follow the example and teachings of Jesus and worship God in the way Jesus taught.

When people talk about the church they often think about a building where Christians meet for worship and other activities. Since the building is usually the central meeting place of a group of Christians in a district, it is one good place to go if you want to find out something about them.

This book is about **St. George's Church** in Letchworth. It is part of the Church of England. Letchworth, the first Garden City, is a medium sized town in Hertfordshire. St. George's Church serves a large housing estate on the outskirts. Many churches are dedicated to a saint. St. George is the patron saint of England and legends say that he was a brave Christian.

THE CHURCH OF ENGLAND

You will find a Church of England parish church in most cities, towns and villages of England. The history of the Church of England in this country can be traced back to at least the 4th century AD. In the time of Henry VIII, the English Church broke away from the main Catholic Church and no longer accepted the Pope in Rome as its leader. The history of how this branch of the Church came into being and grew is most interesting.

As people from England travelled round the world, they took with them their way of worshipping God. So branches of the Church of England grew up in other countries. These usually have a different name, like the Church of Ireland, or the Protestant Episcopal Church of the United States of America. But one name which is often given to all of them is the **Anglican Church**. There is now a world-wide family of Anglican Churches and some of them have united with other branches of the Christian Church.

To find out about a church you need to meet the people who make up that church. In this book you will meet some of the

3

people of St. George's. Visiting an empty church building cannot tell you everything about that church because you do not see and hear what actually happens in it. It is rather like visiting a factory when no one is at work. It would be hard to imagine what a working day is like. But the building can be an interesting place to start your investigations and the church notice board may tell you all sorts of things about a group of Christians. What can you tell about St. George's from the **notice board**?

Finding out about St. George's will help you to understand more about the Anglican Church near you. It will not be exactly the same but you will find many similar things. It is impossible for one book to tell you everything about a church. All through this book you are asked to think about things that Christians do and say. You will need to look for an answer to some of the questions yourself. You may find the answer in an encyclopedia or other book. You may have to ask several people before you are satisfied that you have found the correct answer. There are sometimes several answers to the same question.

2.Why is there a Church in this place?

St. George's Church was opened in 1964, but there have been Anglicans in that area since at least the time of the Doomsday book of 1086. This part of Letchworth stretches out to the little village of Norton where there is an old village church. But the village church was right on the edge of Letchworth away from where most people lived. So the Anglicans built a small hall in the centre of the houses. They used this for worship and other activities. As time went on a new housing estate was built nearby and many more church goers moved into the area. On Sundays the small hall was packed and the people decided to put up a larger building which would be used just for worship.

They consulted the **Bishop** of St. Albans who is responsible for all the Anglican churches in Hertfordshire and Bedfordshire, and finally it was agreed to go ahead. They wanted a building which would tell everyone in the district that there was a group of Christians in that area who worshipped God regularly and cared about that part of Letchworth. So they asked an architect to design a modern building which would be a landmark in the area and tell people something about the beliefs of those who worshipped there.

THE CHURCH ON THE HILL

St. George's stands out as a landmark, because it is on the brow of a hill and because it has a concrete spire, 40 metres high, which can be seen from all round the district. Notice how many old churches are built on the tops of hills and have a tower or spire so that they stand out. Why do you think this is?

Behind the spire there is one **bell** which rings before services: older Anglican churches often have a set of bells (called a peal) which can be heard for several miles. Bells are very expensive today and it would have cost far too much for St. George's to have a set of bells. One bell is enough to let the district know that a service is beginning. The word **service** is short for 'service of worship'. Christians believe that one way they should serve God is by worshipping him.

Many churches are surrounded by a **graveyard**. This link between past and present speaks of the Christian belief in life after death. There is no graveyard on the St. George's site, probably because there is no room and perhaps also because the custom in towns these days is to bury the dead in cemeteries or to cremate them. Remember that an old graveyard can tell you about the past; about people's beliefs, about how they lived, about various diseases that they suffered, and about how rich or poor they were.

The site of St. George's is bordered by two roads. The architect made good use of the shape of the site provided, by designing a church with seating in a semi-circle. This means that everyone can see and hear what is happening. They can also see each other which gives them a feeling of togetherness.

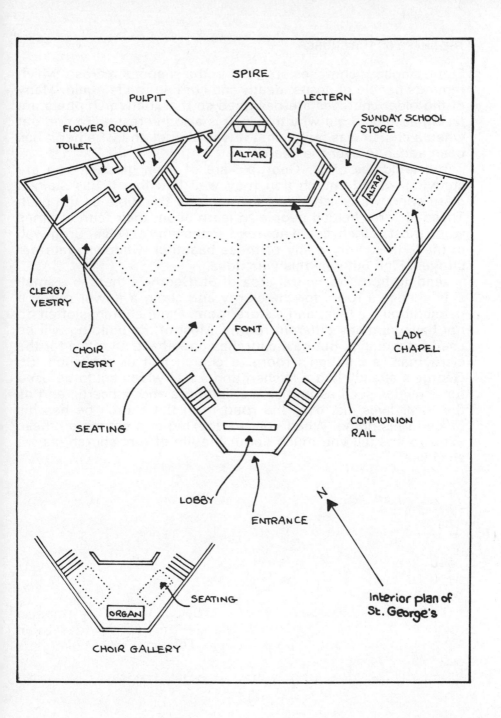

Interior plan of St. George's

THE SHAPE OF THE CHURCH

Some Anglican churches are built in the shape of a cross, which reminds people of Jesus' death and coming to life again. Many of the older churches are designed so that the worshippers are facing east. Find out why this is. It is also interesting to find out when a church was built, what it was built of and whether it has been added to over the years.

The **windows** of St. George's are of plain glass. If you are studying an old church you may well find that it has stained glass windows which show scenes from the Bible or the past. These pictures helped people to learn about their faith in times when most of them could not read. In the time of Oliver Cromwell in the 17th century many of these beautiful windows were destroyed. Find out why this was done.

Leading from the central area of St. George's there is a small side chapel, a room for the clergy and choir, a flower room, a parish library, a toilet and a store room. Older churches often do not have so many different rooms. Most of the building will be used for worship. But new churches often have an office for the clergyman, a children's room, a church hall or a kitchen. St. George's already had a kitchen and a hall which could be used for activities such as parties, conferences and concerts, and as the Vicar lives just over the road from the church he has his office in his home. When you are looking at a church all these extra rooms tell you much about the life of that church, as we shall see.

3. How the Church buildings are used

FIRST IMPRESSIONS ON ENTERING

You go into a church through the **porch**. The porch in St. George's is quite large so that people can linger there to chat after a service. You will find a bookcase with books to buy and to borrow. On one wall there is a large notice-board.

A friendly chat in the porch after a service.

As you climb up the stairs into the **main building** of St. George's, you are struck by its simplicity. It is good to pause on the threshold of any church and think about the feeling it gives you. In an old church you may get a sense of its age and think of how people have worshipped there for hundreds of years.

St. George's is built of brick and concrete and is not plastered or painted inside or outside. It is plain because the worshippers asked the architect to make it so. They wanted this church to say something about their idea of Christianity. **Jesus** led a simple life among poor people and he taught his followers that the most important things in life could not be bought with money. They are things which people can freely give to each other like friendship, care and love. The people in Letchworth wanted their church to teach this truth about Jesus and about Christianity. It is not about riches or position but about the ordinary, simple things of life. The building materials are the ones used in the homes and factories of Letchworth.

The Vicar thinks that if the church building was being put up in the 1980's there would be three main differences. The first is

The figure of Jesus reminds you of his death and resurrection.

that the building would not be so large; the second that it would be adaptable so that it could be used as a hall; and the third that it would probably be shared with several denominations such as the Baptists, Methodists and Roman Catholics.

Dominating the whole church is a huge **figure of Jesus** with a cross behind it. This figure hangs over the **altar** or communion table at the front. The figure reminds you of how Jesus died on the cross on Good Friday (Mark 15: 22–37). But it also reminds you of the belief that Jesus came to life again on Easter Day (Luke 24: 1–6). This figure of Jesus stands out as the most important object in this church. Christians believe that Jesus was the most important person who ever lived. They believe that following Jesus and his teaching is the way we should live our lives. The large figure of Jesus in St. George's is really saying this to all who go into that building.

THE SANCTUARY

Below the figure of Jesus is the area of the church called the sanctuary. Usually only the clergyman and those helping him go into this part of the church. The word 'sanctuary' means 'holy place'. In the sanctuary there is the altar, or table, on which the bread and wine are placed at the Holy Communion Service. The word **altar** means 'high' and it is often set at the top of several steps so that everyone can see it.

THE FONT

This is a large container which holds the water for baptism. A person becomes a member of the Church by being baptised. For this reason the font often stands near the door of a church, to show that a Christian enters the church through baptism.

As you walk into St. George's you will see the black concrete font right in the centre at the back. Not only is it central but it is built around the column which supports the church roof. The architect was trying to show that a person is built into the Christian Church, and becomes part of it when he is baptised. Remember the word 'church' means both a group of people and the building in which they meet.

The word font comes from the same word as fountain, a source

The church is always open for people to use for prayer.

of water. In some churches there are extremely old fonts, nearly a thousand years old, with ancient patterns engraved on them.

PEWS

Modern churches often have seats so that they can be arranged in different ways for various occasions, but St. George's has long benches with backs called pews. They are placed so that the congregation is very much gathered round as a family and no one feels left out in a distant back seat. Wherever you sit you can see everyone else. Many pews in old churches are beautifully carved and in the past people often used to have their own special pew, the wealthy people at the front and the poor people at the back. What do you think about this custom? Do you know of any church where it still happens? Usually today the only people who have a special seat are the church wardens who help in church organisation, the clergyman who conducts the service, and the choir.

HASSOCKS

There are hassocks (or cushions) hanging along the backs of the pews at St. George's. People **kneel** on these when they **pray**. Kneeling to pray is a custom which goes back thousands of years. It is probably linked with kneeling to give homage to a king. The king's subject bowed to show that he was less important. As God was believed to be more important than all earthly kings, Christians bowed down or knelt before him when they talked to him or prayed. Usually these days people will stand to sing or say hymns of **praise**; sit to listen to the Bible being read or to a sermon, and kneel for prayers of **confession** (saying one is sorry for wrong doing) and **intercession** (praying for other people). But churches have different customs so a newcomer needs to watch carefully to find out just what a **congregation** (group of worshippers) does. If a person wishes to sit to pray for some reason, nobody will mind.

CANDLES

Candles are used at most of the services at St. George's. The candles on the Communion table (or altar) are lit for most of the

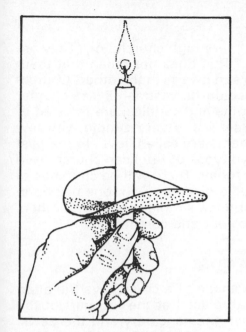
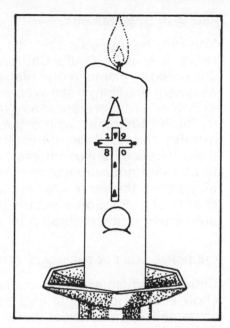

Candles play an important part in church services.

services. The **servers** (people who help the Vicar at services) also carry two extra candles up to the altar for a Communion Service. Light, being the opposite of darkness, symbolises both goodness and truth, and as fire burns up what is bad, it symbolises purity.

Baptism Candle When a child is made a member of the church at baptism (see page 28), a small lighted candle is often given to the parents. This is a sign that a Christian's life should shine out as a candle shines out in the darkness (see Matthew 5:15, 16).

The **Paschal Candle** is a large candle burnt at Easter time. A server lights it for all the services for forty days from Easter Day to Ascension Day (the day Jesus returned to heaven), reminding Christians that Jesus, the light of the world, was seen again by his followers after his resurrection. Into this candle are pressed five studs reminding believers of the five wounds which Jesus received at his crucifixion on Good Friday. The word paschal also links with the Jewish feast of Passover when Jesus was put to death.

HIGH AND LOW CHURCH

You may hear people say, 'It's a very high church,' or, 'They are rather low at St. Paul's Church.' This does not mean that there is a breed of giants in one place and dwarfs in the other! Churches where the clergyman wears colourful vestments (see chapter 4) and where there are many lights and candles, are referred to as 'high'. Churches where the service is very simple with few candles and no elaborate vestments are called 'low'. In the past the difference between these two types of Anglican church used to be more noticeable than it is today. There will be churches of all types in the same area (called a diocese), with one bishop in charge of them. Some people prefer a simple service and others are helped in their worship by colour and ceremony.

CHURCHES BUILT IN THE SHAPE OF A CROSS

Churches which are built in the shape of a cross have the altar, choir stalls and clergyman's stall placed at the top part of the cross called the **chancel**, between the sanctuary and the pews. This section was often divided from the rest of the church by a screen with an archway in the centre. Your local church may

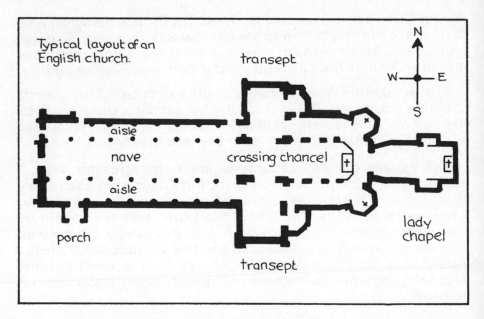

Typical layout of an English church.

N
W — E
S

transept

aisle
nave
crossing chancel
aisle

porch

transept

lady chapel

have an old screen with carvings on it. The part of the church where the congregation sit is called the **nave**. In the arms of the cross there are often small side chapels, children's corners or rooms called vestries where the choir and clergyman robe.

STALLS, LECTERN AND PULPIT

The **Clergymen's Stalls** at St. George's are raised a little above the other pews and at right angles to them. This is so that the clergy can be seen and heard by all. There are two stalls facing each other and they are each side of the sanctuary.

The **Lectern** is a reading desk for the Bible. This is placed in a prominent position in front of the pews so that everybody can see the Bible and hear it being read. The **Bible** is the most important book in the church and is read at every service. In an Anglican church care is taken so that the worshippers hear all the most important parts of the Bible during the year, as the Christian faith is built on Bible teaching. Beside the Bible on the lectern there is usually a little book called a lectionary. This book gives a list of the Bible passages for the morning and evening services on each day of the year. Look to see which translation of the Bible is being used. It may be the old Authorised Version

The designs of the lectern and pulpit are similar.

of 1611 or it may be a modern translation like the New English Bible or the Jerusalem Bible. Many people find the modern translations easier to understand but you will find that some people who know the Authorised Version better prefer that.

The **Pulpit** is a raised platform with a reading desk on it. During the service, the Vicar, or some specially invited visitor, goes into the pulpit and speaks to the congregation for about ten to fifteen minutes as a way of teaching them. His talk is called a **sermon**, and he often refers to the Bible, and helps the people understand what it means to be a Christian today. This talking to the people is also called **preaching** and so the Vicar can be called a preacher.

THE CHOIR

Singing has always been an important part of Christian worship. Congregations sing **psalms** from the Bible and **hymns**. Some of these hymns have been passed down from the early days of Christianity, and were first written in Latin or Greek. In the early days worshippers sang without musical instruments, but instruments of all kinds have been used in church. Since the Middle Ages the organ has been the instrument most commonly used. When you are looking at a church find out which hymn-book is used. It is interesting to see the variety of subjects covered by the hymns. New hymns are regularly being added as books are revised and there are many new hymn-books. St. George's uses *Ancient and Modern Revised* and *100 Hymns for Today*.

The choir lead the rest of the congregation in singing. They practise at least once a week so that they know the hymns and psalms for each service. In St. George's the choir supports the singing from the back. The organ and choir stalls are on a balcony over the porch. In most churches the choir stalls are between the sanctuary and the congregation. Choir members usually wear a cassock and surplice as a uniform (see page 24).

SIDE CHAPELS

Side chapels have a small altar and a few chairs or pews in them. Old churches may have several chapels dedicated to different saints. Important people were often buried under the floors of these chapels and you may find brasses over their tombs or the actual tomb may be erected at the side of the chapel.

19

The lady chapel is used for small gatherings and private prayer.

Lady Chapels are the most common side chapels. Sometimes they are at the east end of a church or cathedral. A lady chapel is one dedicated to Jesus' mother, Mary, and usually has a blue cloth over the altar. This is the colour associated with Mary.

St. George's lady chapel is at the side of the church and is divided from the main church by a curtain. It is quite small (holding about 40 people) and has a small altar. Into this altar is built a stone from a church in New Guinea to which the St. George's congregation is linked. As the church also has links with a church in Africa they have been presented with a crucifix (the figure of Jesus on the cross) carved by a Zulu boy and this is on the wall at the entrance to the chapel.

Towards the front of the chapel is a figure of Mary carved in wood, and in the sanctuary there is a lamp burning. This **sanctuary lamp** hangs in front of a small cupboard in the wall, called an **aumbry**. In this cupboard is kept some bread and wine from the Communion Service and some oil. These may be used when the Vicar visits sick people who are confined to bed. He can bless them by laying his hands on them and putting the sign of the cross on them with oil. He also gives them the bread and wine which have been blessed. The sanctuary lamp burns day and

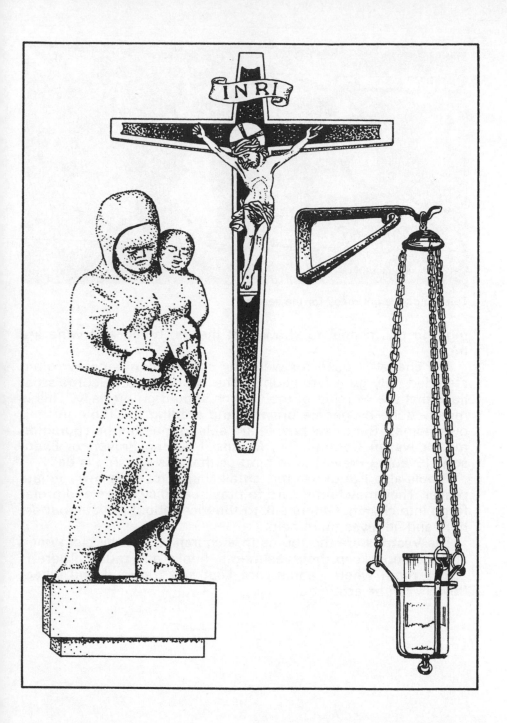

The choir boys get ready for the service.

night in this chapel to show that the oil, bread and wine are there.

The chapel is used for weekday communion services, often attended only by a few people. The people at St. George's believe that the worship of the Church should go on daily. This is mostly done by people praying and reading the Bible in their own homes. But a few people are able to meet in the church on most days for Communion, Matins (Morning Prayer) or Evensong (Evening Prayer) to remind us that this worship is daily.

People also like to use this small chapel for their own private prayer. They may find it hard to pray in a noisy home and prefer to go into church. Others talk to the Vicar about private matters here and he gives them help.

The **Vestries** are the rooms in a church where the clergymen and the choir keep their vestments, books and music. There is also a room where candles are kept and trimmed and where flowers can be arranged.

4. The Vicar and his work

There is a **priest** in charge of every Anglican church. He may be called **Vicar** or Rector. The priest at St. George's is called the Vicar. In some churches there is a second priest who is known as a **curate**. Another name for a priest is a clergyman.

A priest has about three years training for his work. He learns about the Christian faith and also learns to work with people of all ages. After his training he is **ordained** by the bishop. At an ordination the bishop and other clergymen lay their hands on the man's head, and pray for God's Holy Spirit to give him strength for his work.

The Vicar's job is to take the services in the Church, preach and teach the faith and care for his congregation and local community. He is not meant to do all this by himself but to lead the whole congregation to teach and care for other people. He encourages the Christians he works amongst to do the things they are good at. So you may find people looking after little children, say in a play-group, visiting the sick or aged in the area, running a youth club or leading in a Bible study group. They also preach at services and help to plan the life of the Church.

A clerical collar is part of the Vicar's 'uniform'.

SPECIAL CLOTHES

Like clergymen in many churches the Vicar often wears a **clerical collar**. This collar comes from the 1800s when men wore a single neckerchief (rather like huntsmen today). This style gradually changed into a collar and tie. As clergymen in those days were meant to wear a simple white neckerchief this changed into a simple white collar fastened at the back and worn with something black or grey.

When taking a service the Vicar tends to look even more different, for he wears a kind of uniform (rather as a policeman's uniform shows that he is an upholder of the law).

Over his ordinary clothes he wears a **cassock** which is just a long black coat. When he is taking the morning and evening service he will put a **surplice** over his cassock. The word surplice means 'over a fur garment' and this white linen garment with long sleeves was invented to keep out the cold in the winter when churches were not heated. Clergymen sometimes had fur cassocks underneath. Over his surplice he wears a long black scarf. Down his back is a coloured hood which shows he is a man of learning. Some clergymen take the Communion Service wearing a cassock and surplice but they often put on a different coloured scarf, which is called a **stole**.

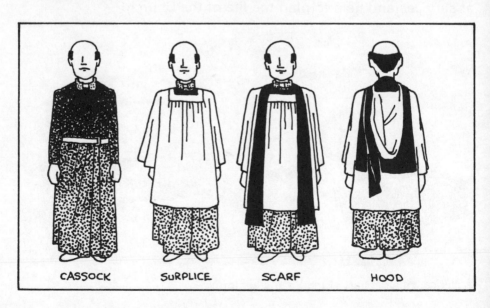

CASSOCK   SURPLICE   SCARF   HOOD

24

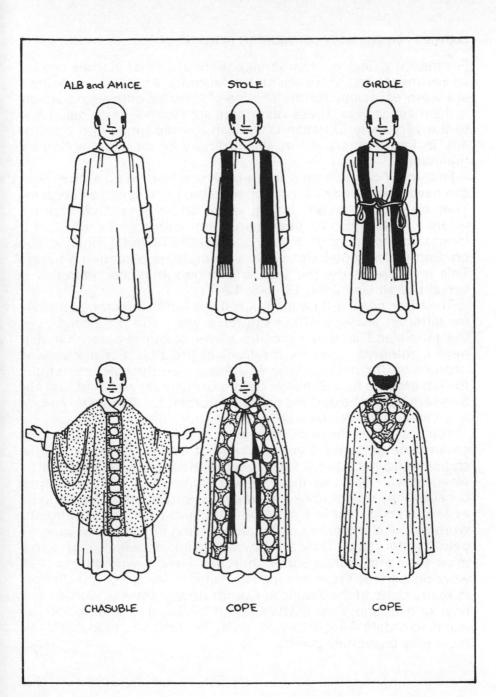

ALB and AMICE

STOLE

GIRDLE

CHASUBLE

COPE

COPE

CLOTHES FOR THE HOLY COMMUNION SERVICE

For the Holy Communion Service there are other clothes known as **vestments** and these are more elaborate. At St. George's they are worn especially for the service of Parish Communion which is the main service. These vestments are clothes which date back to the very early Christian Church in Roman times (4th century AD). In fact they started as the ordinary clothes that a Roman man wore.

First the Vicar puts on a white neck scarf called an **amice**. This can have a coloured collar attached to the back, called an **apparel**. Then he puts on an **alb**, a long white under-tunic. Over that he wears a **stole** which he ties against him with a **girdle** which is a long, thick, white cord. Finally a **chasuble** or outer cloak is put on. Some clergymen also wear a **maniple** representing a towel. This is worn on the left arm and shows that the wearer is a servant of all (see John 13: 4–5, 12–17).

The Vicar has a different coloured chasuble, apparel, and stole for different seasons of the Church's year, and the cloths over the pulpit and lectern have the same colour. Some churches have a coloured cover for the front of the altar. For the festival seasons of Christmas, Easter and Ascension the colour is white; for Advent (the four Sundays before Christmas) and Lent (the six Sundays before Easter) the colour is purple; for Trinity the colour is green and for Whitsun red.

You may think these clothes seem rather strange but they are easier to understand if you know what each one means. Some churches do not have a set of vestments for their clergyman to wear, maybe because they are expensive, but more probably because they do not think they are very important. Other churches like to keep their link with the past, and think that vestments worn by the clergyman and those assisting him help the congregation to worship. They are obviously not necessary but some think they are useful. Some churches have a woman minister working with the Vicar: she may be called a Deacon or Deaconess. In many parts of the Anglican Communion overseas women are now priests and Vicars. The Church of England has decided it wants to ordain women as well, so by the time you read this book there may be women priests.

5. Services of worship

All the main services of worship in the Church of England were written down in the *Book of Common Prayer* in 1662. Recently the language of these services has been modernised and a new prayer book called the *Alternative Service Book* was published in 1980. You may find both books being used in the church you are exploring.

St. George's congregation, like other Anglicans all over the country, follows these services throughout the year. The main prayers, Bible readings, and psalms are given in the Prayer Book but suitable hymns are added. Although all Anglicans follow set services each congregation has its own way of organising worship.

ATTENDING SERVICES

People of all ages go to services at St. George's. They usually go on a Sunday. Do you know why this is? They go to at least one service and sometimes two.

The worshippers arrive at the church building a few minutes before the service. They are greeted and handed a hymn-book and a Prayer Book by a sidesman. Sidesmen can be men or women, and children help as well. After a friendly nod to those around them they usually sit or kneel to say a quiet prayer. Before the service starts the Vicar gives out notices of meetings and activities for the coming week. These are printed on a sheet of paper so that everyone can take one home as a reminder. When the clergymen and choir enter from the vestry everyone stands and the service begins.

BAPTISM

A person is baptised by another Christian sprinkling water over his head, making the sign of the cross on his forehead, and saying his name and, 'I baptise you in the name of the Father and of the Son and of the Holy Spirit.' A person can be baptised at any age. Most Anglican parents like to have their babies baptised because they believe that all people however young can be members of the Church. The word baptise means to dip. In warm countries people are dipped in rivers to be baptised.

Water is used because it is used for washing. When adults are baptised the act of baptism represents the washing away of one way of life and the starting of a new one. Water also gives us life; we would die without it, so the water shows the new way of life which the believer will live. The new way of life is the one which Jesus lived and described.

Baptism took place in Bible times. Jesus was baptised by John the Baptist (Mark 1: 7–11). Later Jesus told his disciples to baptise new believers (Matthew 28: 19–20). So baptism became the way of becoming a Christian (Acts 2:41).

When a baby is baptised the parents state that they believe the teachings of the Church and promise to bring their child up in a Christian way. A baby also has god-parents who make these promises and are meant to help the parents to bring the child up as a Christian.

The baptism of a baby is sometimes called a **christening** be-

At a baptism water is sprinkled over the baby's head.

cause this is the time when the baby is given his Christian name. Some baptism services take place on a Sunday afternoon with just a small family group, but many churches prefer to have the baptism in the middle of the main service on Sunday. They believe that the whole congregation should be there to welcome the newcomers into the Church and promise to look after them. At St. George's if a baby has been baptised with only the family present he is then welcomed into the congregation at the Parish Communion.

CONFIRMATION

This is a service closely linked with baptism. When a baby is baptised the parents and god-parents state that they believe in God and will bring the child up to believe in God and follow Jesus. When the child is old enough to understand what this is all about, he has to decide for himself if he wants to remain a Christian. If he does then he has to state that he believes the teaching of the Church and that he promises to follow Jesus. This takes place at a confirmation service when a person makes his promises before a bishop. The bishop puts his hands on the person's head and says a prayer. Anglicans pray that the person who is confirmed may be strengthened by God's Holy Spirit when the bishop's hands are laid on him.

If there are groups of young people being confirmed at St. George's the bishop may visit the church. Often the confirmation candidates go to the Cathedral in St. Albans to a large service when many people are confirmed.

If an adult becomes a Christian he is often baptised and confirmed on the same day. You can find both these services in the *Alternative Service Book* (1980) and *Book of Common Prayer* (1662).

THE HOLY COMMUNION SERVICE

The Holy Communion Service is the most important service in the Anglican Church. You may find that this service is called the **Eucharist** (pronounced you-kerist) in some churches, as it often is at St. George's. This word means 'thanksgiving' and is the name used by the early Christians. At this service the worshippers remember the Last Supper which Jesus had with his disciples in an upper room. If you read Matthew 26: 17–19, 26–28

Reading from the Gospel in the centre of the church.

The Vicar takes the bread and wine and speaks some of Jesus' words.

and 1 Corinthians 11: 23–26 in the Bible you will find out what Jesus said about the bread and wine.

At St. George's they have the Eucharist as the main service each Sunday and on special days like Christmas Day (the day on which Jesus' birth is celebrated, see Luke 2: 1–20), and Maundy Thursday, (the day of the Last Supper, see Matthew 26: 20–29). A modern version of the service is used.

During the service hymns and psalms are sung and prayers are said and sung; there are at least two readings from the Bible, one of which always comes from one of the four Gospels. The reading from the Gospel is about the life and teaching of Jesus. This is the most important reading in the service. At St. George's the Vicar and servers walk out of the sanctuary and stand in the middle of the congregation for this reading. Then there are prayers of confession, intercession and thanksgiving and usually the Vicar will preach a sermon.

About half way through the service, a small procession of people walk from the back of the church to the sanctuary. They carry the bread and wine for the communion and the plate with money on it. This is how the worshippers show that they offer their lives and work to God. It is called the **offertory**.

The climax of the service comes when the Vicar takes the bread and wine and speaks the words which Jesus used at the Last Supper. Then everyone goes up to the altar step and kneels down. Those who have been confirmed receive bread and wine. Children and those not yet confirmed are blessed by the Vicar who lays his hands on their heads.

The Vicar may have a member of the congregation with him to help give out the bread and wine, especially if the congregation is large. The bread is carried on a paten. **Paten** is the Latin for dish. The wine is put in a chalice. **Chalice** is the Latin for a cup. Many of the names of the objects in a church come from Latin, like font or pew, or from Greek, like Eucharist. These were the earliest languages used by Christians.

The bread used at St. George's is a small round white wafer not like the ordinary bread we eat. These wafers are unleavened bread (made without yeast) similar to that used by Jesus at the Last Supper. But many churches use ordinary bread which has often been baked by a member of the congregation. St. George's

Members of the congregation kneel to receive the bread and wine.

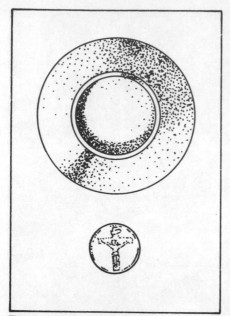

The bread is carried on a paten and the wine is put in a chalice.

does this sometimes, especially for the Harvest Festival. Each person takes a sip of wine from the chalice. By drinking from one cup they show their unity. Christians believe that when they eat the bread and drink the wine at this service, they are close to God in a special way and united with each other and with all believers round the world and throughout history. It is interesting to ask members of the congregation what they feel about this service because you will be given many different answers. If you put these answers together they will give you some idea of the importance of this service.

OTHER SERVICES

Some churches have Morning Prayer at 11.00 a.m. and Evening Prayer at 6.30 p.m. on Sundays as their main services. These services, usually called **Matins** and **Evensong** can be found in the *Alternative Service Book* (1980) and the *Book of Common Prayer* (1662). Both services consist of prayers, Bible readings, psalms and usually hymns and a sermon. The people of St. George's have Evensong on Sundays.

The children put together a Christmas crib which is placed in the church.

At **Christmas** there is the service called Midnight Mass. This is a Communion Service held at midnight on Christmas Eve. Why do you think this service is held in the middle of the night? St. George's also has a service of carols and lessons telling the story of Jesus' birth. This is a special family service. In many churches the children take toys to church at this service. These are given to other children who have no one to give them Christmas presents. A crib scene is usually placed somewhere in the church. The children enjoy helping to put this together.

Palm Sunday On the Sunday commemorating Jesus' entry into Jerusalem on a donkey (Mark 11: 1–11) palm crosses are given to everyone in church. These are small crosses made of strips of palm leaves. They remind the congregation of the palm branches laid on the road by the people of Jerusalem as a carpet for Jesus to ride on. The shape of the cross is a reminder that Good Friday,

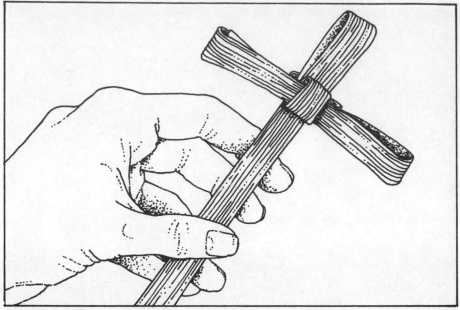
Palm crosses are given to remind people that Jesus died on a cross.

when Jesus died on a cross, is near.

Good Friday On this day St. George's usually has a service where the story of the crucifixion of Jesus is read. This service lasts for three hours to remind the worshippers of the last three hours Jesus hung on the cross. This service includes readings, hymns, prayers and several short talks and times of silence. This is a solemn day and the church is made bare for the occasion. There are no flowers or coloured hangings and the Vicar wears his black cassock without a surplice and scarf.

Easter is marked by a very important Eucharist to celebrate joyously Jesus' resurrection from the dead. A model of an Easter Garden is placed in the church with an empty tomb and three empty crosses in the background. There is much colour and special singing. The church is specially decorated with spring flowers.

Harvest Festival is a thanksgiving to God for the harvest. At this time people bring food into the church, especially fruit and vegetables from the garden. They sometimes take other things which are connected with their work (fishermen take fishing nets, miners take coal).

Weddings Marriages often take place in St. George's on a Saturday. Anyone who lives in the parish of St. George may be married in this Church and people often come to Church for this important ceremony. The couple being married stand in front of the altar and promise before God to love and care for each other for the rest of their lives. They then exchange rings as a sign that they have made these promises.

Funerals When a parishioner dies his coffin is sometimes brought into the Church for a service before being taken to the cemetery or to the crematorium. In the sermon the Vicar will speak about the person's life and give thanks for it.

6. Organising the Church

Each Anglican Church is in a diocese which is a large area like a county. A bishop is in charge of all the churches in one diocese and he helps to choose a clergyman for each church.

The bishops and other clergymen are not the only people who organise the church, for all the church members also have a part to play. They elect a group of about 15 to 20 people, who are called the Parochial Church Council. It is this group which helps the vicar in the daily running of the church. They discuss all that the church is doing, money matters, social activities, services and so on. The congregation also elect **Church Wardens** who take special responsibility for the running of the church.

The Parochial Church Council discuss the running of the church.

Each church sends representatives to a larger meeting called the **Deanery Synod**. There may be twenty or thirty churches represented at a Deanery Synod. This Synod in turn sends representatives to the **Diocesan Synod** which discusses matters of concern to the whole diocese. Finally each diocese sends its bishop, archdeacon (a clergyman who helps the bishop) and six representatives to the **General Synod of the Church of England** which meets in London and York each year. This Synod debates matters which affect the whole Church of England, like the re-writing of the church services and the training of the clergy. So although the bishops are the key people in charge of each section of the church, the rest of the people in the church have a part to play as well.

STEWARDSHIP

As you enter St. George's you will see a notice about stewardship. Stewardship is concerned with the **time**, **talents** and **money** of the people in the congregation. The Church members think how they can help the rest of the Church and other people in the community. They decide how their time should be divided up,

time for work
time for doing what they like
time for worship, prayer and Bible study
time for their families
time for helping others

People give money in special envelopes or place it on the collection plate.

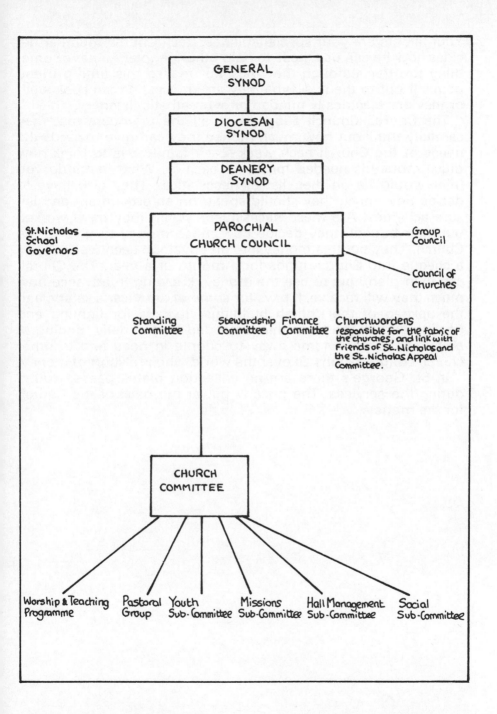

GENERAL SYNOD

DIOCESAN SYNOD

DEANERY SYNOD

St. Nicholas School Governors

PAROCHIAL CHURCH COUNCIL

Group Council

Council of Churches

Standing Committee

Stewardship Committee

Finance Committee

Churchwardens responsible for the fabric of the churches, and link with Friends of St. Nicholas and the St. Nicholas Appeal Committee.

CHURCH COMMITTEE

Worship & Teaching Programme

Pastoral Group

Youth Sub-Committee

Missions Sub-Committee

Hall Management Sub-Committee

Social Sub-Committee

Your talents are your special abilities. Each Church member decides how he can use these to help other people. All have something to offer although they may not realise this until a friend points it out to them. Maybe they are musical or can cook well; or they are electrically minded or sympathetic listeners.

The Church Council suggests to all the members that they carefully think out how much money they can give towards the needs of the Church each week. Each family has to think how much money is needed for its necessities. What items do you think would be on their list of necessities? They also have to decide how much they should spend on entertainment and leisure activities. Are these necessities? When they have worked out their budget, they decide how much money to give to the Church. They put this money into an envelope each week or pay a cheque into Church funds for a month or a year. The Church can then plan how to use the money, knowing in advance how much they will receive. It pays for some of the Vicar's salary, and the upkeep of the Church buildings; it pays for lighting and heating and all the other things needed for the daily running of a church; it gives some away to people in need and to other church congregations all over the world who are short of money.

In St. George's there are no collection plates passed round during the services. The plate is put at the back of the Church for the money.

7. Other Church activities

Attending worship is only part of a Christian's life, and there are many activities which church people do together with other people which are also important. If we look at St. George's this will suggest to you what churches in your area may be doing.

SUNDAY COFFEE

After the Parish Communion on Sunday morning most people go into the hall for coffee and a chat. They call this **Parish Breakfast**. This is a good time to see a friend because most people try to go to this service on Sunday, even if they go to another as well. Everyone catches up with news and arranges other times to meet during the week. Each Sunday a different group of people brews the coffee so that the job is shared. Parish Breakfast helps people to feel that they belong to the family of St. George's. It is also a good time to get to know a newcomer.

The Parish Breakfast is a good time to get to know people.

SOCIAL ACTIVITIES FOR ALL

St. George's has a social committee which arranges several activities for all ages during the year. The Harvest Supper is a regular one and the Parish Outing in the summer is very popular. During the winter there may be a barn dance and perhaps a party. There is also a rambling club which goes for walks in the country. All these relaxed, happy occasions help people to get to know each other well.

The social committee organised this children's party.

MEETING OTHER CHRISTIANS

In Letchworth there are other churches, some Anglican and some of other denominations such as the Free Church, Methodist, Baptist, Roman Catholic, Salvation Army and Quakers. You may find some other churches in your area. The people at St. George's feel it is very important for all the Christians in one place to meet together to worship and discuss their faith and Christian life. Each year there are three services for all the churches, one especially in the **Week of Prayer for Christian Unity** in January, when Christians pray that Christians everywhere might be united. There are also several groups of people from the different churches who meet regularly, to pray, discuss their faith and plan such things as accommodation for homeless people. In many parts of the country groups of churches of different denominations, such as Anglican, Methodist and United Reformed, share one church building and join together for many Sunday services and other activities (see *Visiting a Community Church* in this series).

YOUTH GROUPS

There are the brownies, guides and rangers connected with St.

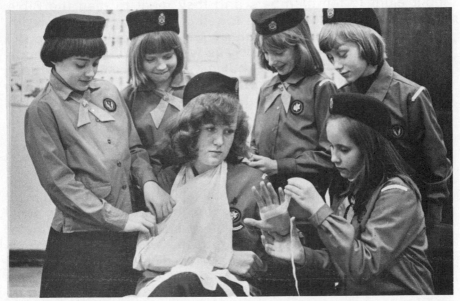

St. George's has an active guide company.

George's. At the moment there are no cub or scout groups. Some of the young people in these groups go to Church with their parents and others don't. On Sundays the young children go to Church with their parents but have their own group to begin with. They join the main Communion Service towards the end. The small ones are looked after by some people who enjoy being with young children. The older ones have Sunday School in the church hall. The teenagers in the Church do not have an organised club. They like to do something for a while and then change, or join in with the older people. Some churches run a Youth Club which any young person in the district can attend, but at the moment St. George's does not do this, as there is already one on the nearby estate. The choir is really a boys' club. They regularly meet to practise and go on outings to sing in other churches. Many churches have girls in the choir as well as boys.

HOUSE GROUPS

In St. George's parish there are about ten small groups of people who meet regularly in each other's homes. These groups have about eight to ten members and they meet to read the Bible, pray and generally to discuss together the things which are important to them. They particularly pray for people who are sick or in trouble, and visit the sick as well. Over the years people join and leave these groups, but most people usually stay long enough to get to know each other very well. It is difficult to know a large congregation well, but in these small groups people feel they have some close friends who are a great help to them.

A WEEKEND AWAY

Sometimes the members of a Parochial Church Council and maybe some other interested people from the congregation go away together for a weekend. They often stay in a house run for conferences by the Diocese. During the weekend they discuss what they should be doing as a church. They might share what the house groups have been doing or plan a campaign to help all the church members think more seriously about stewardship, or organise a method of helping the old and housebound people in the parish. A whole weekend is valuable for talking about such things because a two hour meeting in an evening is always rather rushed. In Letchworth all the Anglican churches share in such weekends and anyone from the congregation can go. They usually think about something which concerns them all and have several services of worship. Such a time is often called **a retreat**.

MEETINGS OF THE CLERGY

The clergymen from all the Anglican churches meet regularly to pray together and discuss their work. They also meet with the clergymen from the other Christian churches so that they can keep in touch with each other's activities and plan things together.

The clergymen of the area meet regularly to discuss and plan activities.

GROUPS FOR MEN AND WOMEN

Some churches have several adult societies like the Mother's Union or a Pensioners' Club or the Church of England Men's Society. The St. George's people do not usually separate in this way as they prefer to do things as families. There is a Women's Fellowship, but the men are often invited to meetings. Most activities have to take place in the evening or at weekends as many men and women are out at work during the day.

THE CHURCH SCHOOL

St. George's has a primary school which is run partly by the Church of England although it is organised in the same way as any other primary school. The people of St. George's take a special interest in this school and are pleased that they have been able to start a nursery unit for very young children.

8. The Church in the community

BEING THE CHURCH EVERY DAY

It is not only on Sundays that the congregation of St. George's is the Church in that area. They are living the Christian life every day of the week at work, at school, at home and at play. They try to care for everyone they meet as Jesus did. They try again cheerfully when they have made mistakes. They try to work hard and be honest in their work. Their worship together and church meetings give them strength to live their daily lives in a Christian way.

LIVING IN LETCHWORTH

Church people get involved in all sorts of activities in their town which they feel are worthwhile. Some St. George's people help run an 'Over Sixties' club which any pensioner can attend. Other churches organise such things as play groups, lunches for lonely

People from St. George's help to run an 'Over Sixties' club and a play group.

people, or hospital visiting. In Letchworth there is a 'Good Neighbour' scheme. This is a way in which people in the same street help each other from day to day. Many church members are involved in this. You will also find St. George's people helping in Citizen's Advice Bureaux, the St. John's Ambulance and the Samaritans. Find out more about these organisations. You may find their names in your local telephone directory.

LIVING IN BRITAIN

Looking further afield many church members support national societies which are helping others, such as the Church of England Children's Society and Shelter, the society which finds accommodation for homeless families. Christians wish to influence Parliament so that fair laws are passed, so they write to their M.P. if they feel strongly on a matter. In their discussion groups church members talk about their country and the way it is governed because this is an important aspect of life.

St. George's has close links with Anglican congregations in Papua New Guinea.

St. George's congregation has a special link with the Anglican Church in **Pakistan** and **New Guinea**. They are visited by people from the churches in these places whenever possible. They pray for them regularly, send money to support special projects and keep in touch by letters. Recently they helped to pay for a priest to be trained in New Guinea. The Bishop of Norwich went to New Guinea for the ordination as the Archbishop's representative. He took with him a cross carved by one of the members of St. George's for the new priest.

Another link with people abroad is through **Christian Aid** which St. George's supports. You will find that many churches support an organisation which is helping the poor and people in distress all over the world. Examples of such organisations are Save the Children, Oxfam, War on Want and Tear Fund. Each year St. George's members help to raise money in Christian Aid week by such things as house-to-house collections, sponsored walks and hunger lunches. This money goes to help people who have lost their homes in earthquakes or hurricanes, or to people who are

trying to improve their standard of living so that they have a proper home, and their children are clothed and fed. (For addresses see the end of this chapter.)

St. George's Church is also a member of the United Nations Association which is another way of keeping in touch with what is happening all over the world and supporting those who are working for justice and peace in every country.

Addresses of Charities
Christian Aid, P.O. Box No. 1, London SW9 8BH
Oxfam, 274 Banbury Road, Oxford
Save the Children, 157 Clapham Road, London SW9 0PT
Tear Fund, 1 Bridgeman Road, Teddington, Middlesex
War on Want, 467 Caledonian Road, London N7 9BE
The United Society for Christian Literature, Luke House, Farnham Road, Guildford, Surrey GU1 4XD

9. Over to you

This book has given you a glimpse into the life of one group of Anglican Christians. St. George's Church is not famous; it is one group of Christians in one part of a medium sized town. It is a group which is changing all the time and as new people arrive and others leave so the life the Church changes. It is a friendly, welcoming Church where the people are finding the Christian faith a very important part of their lives. They sum up their Christian life by saying,

Our purpose as a Church is to
Worship God in Christ,
Discover the meaning of Christian faith today,
Serve humanity – especially our own community.

Anglican churches can look very different.

Find out about the Anglican church in your town or village. Is it like St. George's in some way? How is it different? You may find a friendly, flourishing, lively church or perhaps you will find it is empty and run down and gives you no friendly welcome. It may be in a town centre where few people live so the congregation is very small. The building may be too large and expensive for the people to look after, so it has become dilapidated.

If possible try to visit a church building when some of the members are there. You may be able to go for a service or to a house group. You may be able to meet the Vicar or one of the other church members. You might meet some of the people from a church before you visit their building and this may be helpful.

Record the facts about your church and always look for reasons. Remember you will find out most by talking to the **people** of the church. Perhaps you could arrange a special time to talk to one of the church members or a clergyman.

Build up your picture of a church by recording things you find out. You could keep a notebook for collecting facts and later write them neatly in a file and add sketches or photographs. You may be able to buy a magazine or other booklets about the church activities. If you have a tape recorder you could tape a conversation with a church member about a Bible study group, or ask them why they visit people in hospital or what the Sunday services are like.

If you are studying a church which is an old historical building you will want to look up the history of the building. There are suitable books about this listed at the end of this chapter.

Find out about other Christian Churches in your area and you will discover many similarities to the Church of England in their life and worship.

Over to you!

Book List

Church buildings
P. J. Hunt, *Churches and Chapels*, Watts
H. & R. Leacroft, *Churches and Cathedrals*, Lutterworth
P. J. Hunt, *What to look for inside a church*, Ladybird
P. J. Hunt, *What to look for outside a church*, Ladybird
H. Pluckrose, *Churches*, Mills & Boon
I. Calvert, *Churches in Britain*, Basil Blackwell

History
P. Tilney, *Tudors and Stuarts*, chapters 3 and 4, Mills & Boon

In this series
G. Palmer, *Visiting a Community Church*, Lutterworth
D. Sullivan, *Visiting a Roman Catholic Church*, Lutterworth
D. K. Babraa, *Visiting a Sikh Temple*, Lutterworth
T. Bates, *Visiting a Methodist Church*, Lutterworth
R. Protheroe & R. Meheralin, *Visiting a Mosque*, Lutterworth
M. Blackwell, *Visiting a Salvation Army Citadel*, Lutterworth
D. Charing, *Visiting a Synagogue*, Lutterworth

Index

lady chapel, 20
Last Supper, 32
lectern, 17
lectionary, 17
Lent, 26
light, 15
low church, 16

maniple, 26
marriage, 38
Matins, 22, 34
Maundy Thursday, 32
Midnight Mass, 35
money, 42

nave, 17
New English Bible, 18

offertory, 32
oil, 20
ordination, 23

Palm Sunday, 35
Parochial Church Council, 39
parish breakfast, 43
paschal candle, 15
paten, 32
peal, 6
pews, 14
porch, 9
praise, 14
pray, 14
Prayer Book, 28
preach, 18
priest, 23
psalms, 18
pulpit, 18

Rector, 23
resurrection, 36
retreat, 47

sanctuary, 12, 32
sanctuary lamp, 20

school, 48
sermon, 18
servers, 15
service, 6
sick people, 20, 46
sidesmen, 28
stewardship, 40
stole, 26
surplice, 18, 24
synods, 40

talents, 42
Trinity, 26

unleavened bread, 32

vestments, 26
vestries, 17, 22
Vicar, 23, 26

wafer, 32
wardens, 14, 39
weddings, 38
Whitsun, 26
wine, 20, 32

youth groups, 45